D1528570

AMENDMENTS TO THE UNITED STATES CONSTITUTION
THE BILL OF RIGHTS

THE RIGHTS OF THE ACCUSED IN CRIMINAL CASES

THERESE SHEA

THE SIXTH AMENDMENT

rosen publishing's
rosen central®

New York

Published in 2011 by The Rosen Publishing Group, Inc.
29 East 21st Street, New York, NY 10010

Copyright © 2011 by The Rosen Publishing Group, Inc.

First Edition

Library of Congress Cataloging-in-Publication Data

Shea, Therese.
The Sixth Amendment: the rights of the accused in criminal cases / Therese Shea.
    p. cm. — (Amendments to the United States Constitution: the Bill of Rights)
Includes bibliographical references and index.
ISBN 978-1-4488-1261-5 (library binding)
ISBN 978-1-4488-2307-9 (pbk.)
ISBN 978-1-4488-2319-2 (6-pack)
1. United States. Constitution. 6th Amendment—Juvenile literature. 2. Due process of law—United States—Juvenile literature. 3. Criminal procedure—United States—Juvenile literature. I. Title.
KF45586th .S52 2011
345.73'056—dc22

                                                                        2010021318

Manufactured in the United States of America

CPSIA Compliance Information: Batch #W11YA: For further information, contact Rosen Publishing, New York, New York, at 1-800-237-9932.

On the cover: All Americans, from the most famous and powerful to everyday citizens, have the same rights if they are accused of crimes. The Sixth Amendment states that accused persons have the right to a speedy and public trial, an impartial jury of their peers, and legal counsel. These principles have been applied in the criminal cases of O. J. Simpson (*left*), Mark Hacking (*center*), and Bernard Madoff (*right*).

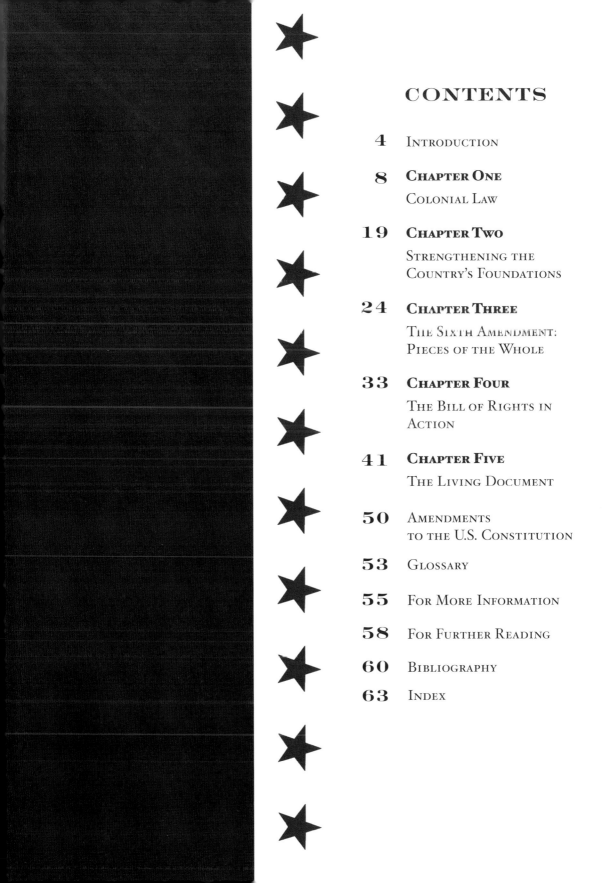

CONTENTS

INTRODUCTION

B ob Granville Pointer was on trial in Texas. He was accused of robbing Kenneth Phillips of several hundred dollars at gunpoint. Phillips testified against Pointer at a hearing before the trial. Phillips moved to California before the actual trial began. However, his testimony from the hearing was given as evidence. Though Pointer was convicted, his defense lawyer argued that Texas courts had denied Pointer his right to confront his accuser. After all, Phillips could not be questioned at the trial about his statements. Was Phillips's testimony at the pretrial hearing enough to convict Pointer? In 1965, the court case *Pointer v. Texas* was heard by the United States Supreme Court, the highest court in the country.

The accused may be handcuffed in court if the judge believes he or she is a threat to others. Still, an accused person retains a number of important rights until he or she is proven guilty.

The right to confront a witness is guaranteed in the Sixth Amendment of the U.S. Constitution. However, at the time of Pointer's trial, this part of the Sixth Amendment applied only to federal trials—not to state trials. The Supreme Court overturned Bob Granville Pointer's conviction. They agreed that his right had not been honored. Following this case, all state courts had to respect the "confrontation clause" in criminal cases.

What does Pointer's case mean to the average person? Chances are, you have never been accused of a major crime. Imagine this: You are called into your principal's office. She says, "I heard you broke those chairs in the lunchroom. I'm going to recommend to the school board that you are thrown out of this school."

"Who told you I did this?" you cry, amazed and confused.

"One of your classmates told us all about it. Consider yourself expelled."

In the United States, we all have certain rights and protections that help us when we are accused of doing wrong. If your principal's office were a court of law, your principal would have to honor the confrontation clause of the Sixth Amendment. She would have to let you confront your accuser, your classmate, and any other witnesses against you. This protection helps anyone who is charged with a crime prove his or her innocence. Additional protections for the accused make up the remainder of the Sixth Amendment.

The U.S. Constitution outlines the powers and responsibilities of our government. An amendment is a change to the Constitution. Amendments were added, not as afterthoughts, but as carefully considered guarantees of certain rights for U.S. citizens. The Sixth Amendment focuses on the rights of those accused of a crime. It states:

> In all criminal prosecutions, the accused shall enjoy the right to a speedy and public trial, by an impartial jury of the State and district wherein the crime shall have been committed, which district shall have been previously ascertained by law, and to be informed of the nature and cause of the accusation; to be confronted with the witnesses against him; to have compulsory process for obtaining witnesses in his favor, and to have the Assistance of Counsel for his defence.

In one long sentence, the Founding Fathers of our nation explained several ways in which American citizens could expect to be treated fairly in the U.S. court system.

Read the first ten amendments at the end of this book. Together, these amendments are known as the Bill of Rights. Notice how many rights involve people in criminal court cases. The Fourth, Fifth, Sixth, Seventh, and Eighth Amendments give those accused of criminal acts the best possible chance to prove their innocence. Should any citizens be found guilty, they are promised fair treatment.

The early government of the United States devoted much time and effort to creating just laws. The attention to the new judicial (court) system was, in part, a reaction to the negative experiences of the American colonists under British law.

CHAPTER ONE

COLONIAL LAW

I n the years leading up to the American Revolution, the voices of the American colonists became loud with discontent. Up to this point, Great Britain had allowed a certain amount of self-government in the colonies. However, by the 1760s, Britain was writing laws for the colonies and passing them across the Atlantic Ocean. Many colonists thought these laws benefited Great Britain much more than the colonies. Colonial representatives had little power. Instead, officials in London represented their interests in Parliament, Britain's legislative body. Many colonists believed that this "virtual representation" was unjust. They wanted "actual representation," or their own elected leaders to act on behalf of colonial concerns.

Challenging Colonial Law

King George III and his government had colonists seething with anger. The British Parliament passed taxes, such as the Stamp Act of 1765, without the consent of colonial representatives. Colonists actively and openly challenged the Stamp Act, forcing it to be repealed the following year.

However, despite negative reactions in the colonies, laws continued to be enacted and enforced. In fact, the British government tried to tighten its control with more laws to silence opposition. On the same day that Parliament repealed the Stamp Act in 1766, it passed the Declaratory Act. The Declaratory Act stated that Parliament had the "full power and authority to make laws and statutes . . . to bind the colonies and people of America, subjects of the crown of Great Britain, in all cases whatsoever."

Tension between the British government and its colonial subjects gave spark to acts of rebellion. One of the most famous incidents took aim at a tea tax. Colonists, in protest of the tax, had been selling and using smuggled tea from other countries. The British governor of Massachusetts demanded that the people of Boston buy British tea. On the evening of December 16, 1773, a group of men who called themselves the Sons of Liberty gathered at Boston Harbor. Dressed as Mohawk Indians, they boarded three British ships and dumped 340 chests of British tea into Boston Harbor. This event later became known as the Boston Tea Party.

On the heels of this rebellious event, the British Parliament passed the Administration of Justice Act in May 1774. The measure allowed the governor of the Massachusetts colony to move a trial to another colony or even to Great Britain. The act was designed to keep American rebels

on trial from being set free by sympathetic colonial juries. Colonists imagined being transported hundreds of miles away to their deaths in prison. The law was also designed to protect public servants working on behalf of Britain, such as officers putting down a riot. Holding trials in

Of the Boston Tea Party, John Adams wrote, "There is a Dignity, a Majesty, a Sublimity, in this last Effort of the Patriots that I greatly admire."

Great Britain would make it more difficult to try and convict those who committed crimes while doing their jobs. Rather than silence the growing number of colonial rebels, the Administration of Justice Act was labeled an "Intolerable Act" and was considered further reason for defiance.

Thomas Jefferson wrote *A Summary View of the Rights of British America* in 1774. He argued that trying a murder that occurred in Boston in Great Britain was unjust, writing:

> For who does his majesty think can be prevailed on to cross the Atlantic for the sole purpose of bearing evidence to a fact? His expences are to be borne, indeed, as they shall be estimated by a governor; but who are to feed the wife and children whom he leaves behind, and who have had no other subsistence but his daily labour? . . . And the wretched criminal, if he happen to have offended on the American side, stripped of his privilege of trial by peers of his vicinage, removed from the place where alone full evidence could be obtained, without money, without counsel, without friends, without exculpatory proof, is tried before judges predetermined to condemn.

Jefferson pointed out the unfairness of asking witnesses to spend months traveling—in those days by sea—to Great Britain for a trial. Who would want to be a witness and leave one's family and job for so long? He also argued that it was unjust to take the accused away from friends and supporters. Later, Jefferson helped create Virginia's state constitution. The document guaranteed that a criminal trial would be held before "an impartial jury of his vicinage," or a fair jury in one's own community.

British Law Before the Revolution

At first, most colonists did not wish to break away from Great Britain. They thought of themselves as British citizens. However, they wanted true representation in the government. As citizens, they expected to have the rights held by the British for hundreds of years. Not only did colonists have little representation in Parliament, but they had to follow laws that contrasted with British law. When some colonists learned they would be forced to follow a new, unjust law, they cried out, "Magna Carta!"

Magna Carta (1215)

In early thirteenth-century England, King John feared losing his throne. He had made unpopular laws and disastrous military decisions. Noblemen presented him with the Magna Carta, or Great Charter, in 1215. The document outlined certain rights for the English people that even the monarch could not take away. King John agreed to the contents of the charter. He promised that not only he, but also his descendants, would grant "to all freemen of our kingdom" the rights within the document. The Magna Carta placed the ruler of England within the law, rather than above the law.

The original Magna Carta document was copied many times. This manuscript from the Bodleian Library collection in Oxford, England, is one of the earliest, dating from 1217.

One clause of the Magna Carta states, "No freemen shall be taken or imprisoned or disseised [dispossessed] or exiled or in any way destroyed ... except by the lawful judgment of his peers or by the law of the land." The Administration of Justice Act violated these ideas by taking the accused from his peers and community. When the colonists fought the Administration of Justice Act, they fought for a right they believed all British citizens had possessed since King John's rule.

Later, the Magna Carta became an important source for those writing the U.S. Constitution. Similar ideas would appear in a new form in the Sixth Amendment of the Constitution.

The Boston Massacre Trials

One of the most famous trials prior to the American Revolution took place following a deadly incident in 1770. By this time, Boston residents had grown to dislike the constant presence of British soldiers in their city. Anger turned to violence on the night of March 5, 1770. It began with a disagreement between a soldier and a wigmaker. A huge mob of colonists gathered. British captain Thomas Preston assembled a group of eight men to rescue the soldier from the crowd. The colonial mob began throwing snowballs, sticks, rocks, and other objects at the British soldiers. One of the colonists grabbed a soldier's gun. The soldier yelled, "Fire!" Five colonists were killed and another six were injured before Preston called for the shooting to stop.

This event later became known as the Boston Massacre. Some, including Samuel Adams, saw the British as attackers of a peaceful assembly. Adams and others called for British soldiers to be removed from Boston permanently.

In the meantime, colonists demanded justice for the dead. The British soldiers needed legal counsel. John Adams, then a lawyer in Boston, was asked to defend the soldiers. Though many did not want him to take the case, Adams believed everyone had the right to counsel. Adams built a successful defense. Captain Preston was acquitted based on the fact that he had never told his men to fire. Six soldiers, having held fire, were acquitted as well.

Two soldiers had fired their guns. In their defense, Adams told the jury to ask themselves, "What had eight soldiers to expect from such a set of people? Would it have been a prudent resolution in them, or in any body in their situation, to have stood still, to see if the sailors would knock their brains out, or not?"

The jury agreed. The two soldiers were found guilty of manslaughter but were not sentenced to death. Instead, they had the letter "m" branded on their right thumbs: the "m" was for murder. In Adams's words, "As the Evidence was, the Verdict of the Jury was exactly right."

Common Law

Since the Middle Ages, the British courts have practiced common law. Under common law, a court decides a case based on past decisions. Each case becomes part of a massive body of law, which is used in later cases involving similar matters. Judges make similar decisions regarding similar cases. Therefore, trials with like events could be expected to have like conclusions.

However, colonists experienced a departure from common law in their courts before the American Revolution. There are records of merchants tried for smuggling foreign goods in order to avoid paying taxes on British goods. In their trials, the royally appointed judges did not use established common law in their decisions. Rather, they punished merchants based only on Parliament's new laws. Again, the colonists saw these decisions as disregarding their rights as British citizens.

Declaration of Rights

Less than one hundred years before the American Revolution, in 1689, British citizens compiled their rights into a document known as the Declaration of Rights. Sometimes called the English Bill of Rights, the declaration listed thirteen complaints against the actions of King James II, including enacting and suspending laws without Parliament's consent and denying freedom of speech. This declaration announced the end of the reign of King James II and strengthened the rights of the British people. As British colonists in America began to discuss revolution, they held the Declaration of Rights as another defense of their actions. After all, they argued, they were forced to follow laws without their consent and were denied the right to assemble in public to protest.

Government in Revolution

A body of colonial representatives known as the Continental Congress came together to reach a decision about the conflict with Great Britain. The representatives met in Philadelphia in two sessions called the First Continental Congress (1774) and the Second Continental Congress (1775–1781). The First Continental Congress recorded a declaration of the colonists' rights, including life, liberty, property, assembly, and petition. The declaration demanded the repeal of laws that deprived the colonists of trial by jury. It also condemned taxation without representation.

Having failed to reach any agreement with Great Britain and with the colonies now at war, the Second Continental Congress approved the Declaration of Independence on July 4, 1776. The document declared, "These United Colonies are, and of right ought to be, free and independent states." Like the Declaration of Rights of 1689, the Declaration of Independence listed complaints against the British monarch.

The colonists and the British fought the American Revolutionary War until the signing of the Treaty of Paris in 1783. As the war progressed, the Founding Fathers began the task

The First Continental Congress was held in Philadelphia from September to October 1774. Representatives including Samuel Adams, John Adams, George Washington, and Patrick Henry helped to define American rights.

of forming a government for the new nation. The American states had broken from the mother country because of that government's injustices. The leaders needed to create a government that would function on behalf of its citizens' best interests.

By the end of 1777, each colony, now a state, had written a state constitution. Many of the state constitutions were based on the original charters of the colonies. Some included their own statement of independence, not only from Great Britain but also from other states. Several states listed rights for their citizens. Virginia's constitution stated that all men were equal and free. The New York and Maryland state constitutions promised the right to practice religion freely. The Pennsylvania and Vermont constitutions contained the right to free speech.

The next step in the formation of the nation was to unite thirteen separate states. Together, they could trade with other countries, protect themselves from war, and better the lives of all American citizens.

CHAPTER TWO

STRENGTHENING THE COUNTRY'S FOUNDATIONS

The task that lay before the Founding Fathers was not an easy one. At that time, people believed they were citizens of their state. Because of their experience with the British king, many were suspicious of a union headed by a central power. The colonists' experience had shown that a monarchy placed much power in the hands of one person and little power in the hands of the citizens. The Founding Fathers believed the U.S. federal, or central, government could not be allowed the power to violate its citizens' rights. They created a set of rules to guarantee that the federal government would act for the well-being of its citizens.

Two Constitutions

The first constitution of the new nation was called the Articles of Confederation. Though it created the United States of America, it was weak. Under the Articles of Confederation, Congress had little authority. It could not collect taxes to support itself or carry out government programs. Any state that did not agree with Congress could choose not to follow federal laws. The United States needed a stronger plan, and the country's leaders knew it. In 1787, delegates came together at a Constitutional Convention. Instead of improving the Articles of Confederation, the representatives decided to start over. The United States Constitution is the document they created.

James Madison is sometimes called the Father of the Constitution for his contributions to its contents. As the Articles of Confederation appeared to be failing, Madison studied governments similar to that of the early United States. Thomas Jefferson gave him

James Madison gave credit to many sources when he was hailed as the Father of the Constitution. He said it was not "the off-spring of a single brain," but "the work of many heads and many hands."

"trunk loads" of books to aid him. Madison found examples of unions of states in the histories of ancient Greece, Switzerland, and Germany. He especially focused on the weaknesses and failures of these governments. He found that unions could not survive if states had more power than the central government.

Madison found a model for a federal government in the works of seventeenth-century philosopher John Locke. According to Locke, a central government could be split into parts, or branches, preventing one branch from gaining too much power. Madison concluded that the United States could keep both federal and state governments. However, the federal government had to have power over the states to survive. These concepts were the basis of his Virginia Plan, the frame for the U.S. Constitution. The people who supported this plan were called Federalists. Those who opposed a strong federal government were called Anti-Federalists.

John Locke: Founding Grandfather

English philosopher John Locke lived from 1632 to 1704. He was highly regarded by the Founding Fathers, including James Madison, for his thoughts on representation in government. Locke's writings also provided support for the American Revolution. Locke maintained that revolution is not just a right—sometimes it is a duty to overthrow an unjust government. He also thought that all people were born with "natural rights" and should be free to pursue "life, health, liberty, and possessions."

Thomas Jefferson later used these concepts in the Declaration of Independence: "We hold these truths to be self-evident, that all men are created equal, that they are endowed by their Creator with certain unalienable Rights, that among these are Life, Liberty and the pursuit of Happiness."

A war of words began between the Federalists and Anti-Federalists. In order for the U.S. Constitution to become law, it had to be ratified by nine states. Madison, along with Alexander Hamilton and John Jay, wrote a series of essays in 1787 and 1788 called the Federalist Papers. Eighty-five essays were published in New York newspapers, encouraging the state's representatives to ratify the Constitution.

Rescuing the Constitution with the Bill of Rights

Anti-Federalists feared that the rights of citizens would suffer under the Constitution's federal government. Madison maintained that a central government could actually help to preserve citizens' freedoms, if given enough power. In addition, many state constitutions included individual rights already.

The U.S. Constitution did guarantee certain individual rights. For example, Article III Section 2 states:

The trial of all crimes, except in cases of impeachment, shall be by jury; and such trial shall be held in the state where the said crimes shall have been committed; but when not committed within any state, the trial shall be at such place or places as the Congress may by law have directed.

Here, the Constitution assures the placement of a trial within the community of the crime—the same right that the Administration of Justice Act stripped from the colonists.

Still, some state representatives refused to ratify the Constitution without a listing of Americans' rights. Madison worried that holding another convention to add these rights might open up the entire

Constitution, including the structure of the government, to changes. Rather than allow his plan to be picked apart, he accepted the responsibility of writing the first amendments to the Constitution. Madison presented his proposed amendments in an address to the House of Representatives on June 8, 1789.

James Madison's amendments were not original ideas. They were "known and not new truths," words he would later write in reference to the Declaration of Independence. As with the constitution, Madison took his amendments from writings such as John Locke's philosophical works, the Declaration of Rights

On September 25, 1789, the U.S. Congress proposed twelve constitutional amendments to the state legislatures. The first two amendments were not ratified. Articles three through twelve became known as the Bill of Rights, above.

of 1689, the Magna Carta, the state constitution of Virginia, and the 1776 Virginia Declaration of Rights. Of Madison's proposed amendments, twelve were passed by Congress and sent to the state legislatures for ratification. The states ratified ten of these amendments on December 15, 1791. Known as the Bill of Rights, these ten amendments are listed in the back of the book.

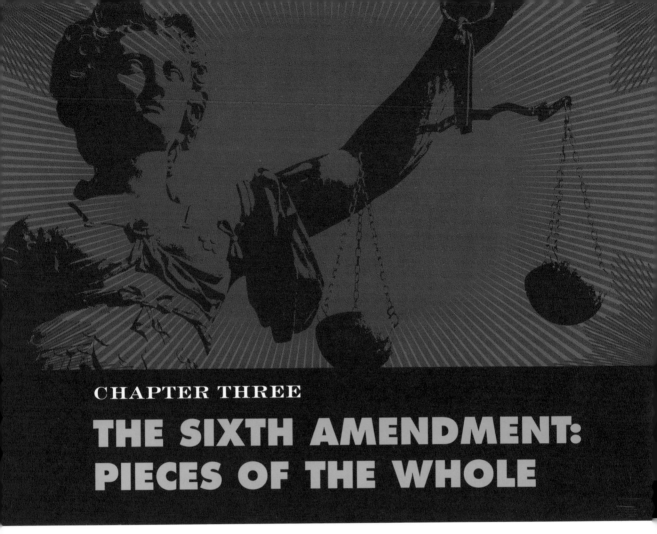

CHAPTER THREE

THE SIXTH AMENDMENT: PIECES OF THE WHOLE

T he U.S. court system recognizes that different crimes need to be addressed by different laws. Civil cases, for example, involve rights and duties among citizens, which are often settled by an exchange of money. Criminal cases, on the other hand, involve crimes against society. The government represents the victims and prosecutes on their behalf. A trial can result in jail time, or even the death penalty, for the person who committed the crime. Since punishments can be severe, the importance of the Sixth Amendment and other rights of the accused is undeniable. The Sixth Amendment contains a number of rights for American citizens in criminal trials. This chapter contains a description of each right.

Speedy and Public Trial

The accused shall enjoy the right to a speedy and public trial

The first part of the Sixth Amendment actually lists two rights: the right to a fast trial and the right to a trial held in public. Without the first right, an accused person could wait years in jail before his or her trial. Delaying a trial is unfair to someone who is actually innocent and is waiting to prove his or her innocence. Evidence may be lost, and witnesses may move away or die. The Supreme Court later established that "speedy" is not a specific amount of time. The courts weigh factors to decide if a delay is unjust. If it is, the defendant or the convicted person may be set free.

Without the right to a public trial, the accused person's trial could be held in secret, without witnesses or friends for support. Secret trials are quite common in history, especially by corrupt governments. Public criminal trials are more likely to be fair, since the community can see whether the proceedings match the outcome. Witnesses may be less likely to commit perjury, or lie under oath, if others are present who can state that they are wrong. Public trials also demonstrate to people that the judicial system is just and effective.

Fair Jury Trial Where the Crime Was Committed

By an impartial jury of the State and district wherein the crime shall have been committed, which district shall have been previously ascertained by law

Trial by jury, rather than by a single judge, was a long-honored tradition in Great Britain before the American Revolution. A judge may be

This 1808 painting shows the Old Bailey, the Central Criminal Court of London. The presence of a jury, as well as the viewing public, is a feature also respected in U.S. courts.

biased against a defendant for any number of reasons. Some defendants are repeat offenders or are hostile in court. Some judges are elected and may be promised support if they make a certain decision in a case. A jury of many citizens is more likely to remain impartial. People may not serve on a jury if they are biased against a subject, organization, or individual involved in a case. Jury candidates are asked questions to determine bias during the jury selection process.

According to the Sixth Amendment, it is also necessary for a trial to take place where the crime was committed and for the jury to be from that area. To further assure impartiality, juries should truly represent the community. For example, a jury should not be made up of only police officers or only wealthy people. Twentieth-century court cases have extended this idea to race and gender.

To Be Told of the Accusation

And to be informed of the nature and cause of the accusation

The accused in the criminal trial has the right to know exactly what he or she is accused of doing. This is the starting point for preparing a defense. If there are many parts of the crime, the accused person must know all of these parts, too. For example, if a person is told he is accused of murder, the person can build a case to show that he is not guilty of murder. If, in the course of the murder trial, someone accuses him of robbery, he does not have to defend himself against the robbery charge, only murder.

To Know and Ask Witnesses Questions

To be confronted with the witnesses against him

A defendant has the right to know who is accusing her. She also has the right to ask the accuser questions. This part of the amendment is called the "confrontation clause." Witnesses must be cross-examined in front of the jury. This helps the jury to better evaluate the witnesses' statements. A witness may seem trustworthy, or the person may seem dishonest. The jury weighs whether or not to believe each witness's testimony.

The right of confrontation protects the accused from hearsay. Statements heard outside of court are called hearsay. Hearsay statements are similar to rumors. They are not part of a witness's personal

An attorney cross-examines, or questions, any witnesses brought by the opposing side. The judge controls the questioning process and rules on issues, such as objections to the questions asked.

experience. For instance, a person may hear another person bragging about robbing a house. The witness to the bragging cannot know if the person was telling the truth. So the bragging is labeled as hearsay. There are exceptions to the hearsay rule. For example, sometimes a witness dies before a trial takes place. Statements the person made before death may be allowed as evidence.

Dying Declarations as Evidence

At the trials following the Boston Massacre, John Adams—the defense lawyer for the British soldiers—wanted to convince the jury that the soldiers had fired on the colonists in self-defense. He submitted as evidence the dying words of Patrick Carr, one of the colonists who had been killed. This evidence is an exception to the hearsay rule. It is called a dying declaration. Here is an account of Adams's questioning of his witness, Dr. John Jeffries, from the Web site of the Boston Massacre Historical Society (http://www.bostonmassacre.net):

Adams: *Was you Patrick Carr's surgeon?*
Jeffries: *I was . . .*
Adams: *Was he [Carr] apprehensive of his danger?*
Jeffries: *He told me . . . he was a native of Ireland, that he had frequently seen mobs, and soldiers called upon to quell them. . . he had seen soldiers often fire on the people in Ireland, but had never seen them bear half so much before they fired in his life . . .*
Adams: *When had you the last conversation with him?*
Jeffries: *About four o'clock in the afternoon, preceding the night on which he died, and he then particularly said, he forgave the man whoever he was that shot him, he was satisfied he had no malice, but fired to defend himself.*

According to Jeffries' testimony, before Carr died, he said the mob was worse than any he had ever seen and that he believed his killer shot in self-defense. The judge accepted this hearsay evidence. He told the jury that because Carr was about to die, he had no reason to lie or to defend the man who had shot him. Carr's words could be viewed as truthful testimony.

Witnesses That Can Help the Defense Must Testify

To have compulsory process for obtaining witnesses in his favor

In British common law, people accused of certain crimes, such as treason, were not allowed to have witnesses speak on their behalf. However, the Sixth Amendment guarantees this right in criminal trials. Just as the accused has the right to question witnesses who offer testimony against him, the accused has the right to question witnesses who can prove his innocence. Perhaps witnesses can testify that the defendant was nowhere

The term "subpoena" means "under punishment" in Latin. It is an order for a person to appear in court. A person can receive a penalty, such as a fine or arrest, for failure to comply.

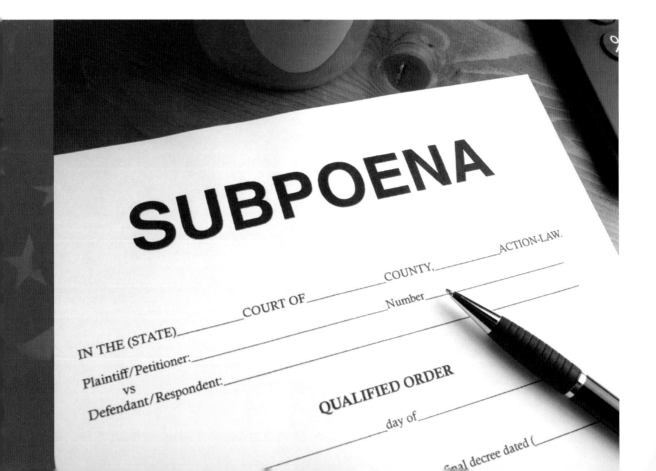

near the crime. Perhaps they can offer evidence that the defendant has good character and is not likely to have committed the crime. A defendant can also take the stand to speak for himself.

Witnesses who are necessary to either the prosecution or the defense are given subpoenas. These are legal orders stating that they must appear in court and submit whatever evidence they have.

Amendment in Action

You have the right to remain silent. Anything you say can and will be used against you in a court of law. You have the right to speak to an attorney, and to have an attorney present during any questioning. If you cannot afford a lawyer, one will be provided for you at government expense.

There are other variations of this speech, called the Miranda warning or Miranda rights.

Police officers once had the ability to question people without a warning. They could then use things that people would say to them as evidence. It was the accused's duty to know his or her rights. However, one case changed all that.

In 1963, Ernesto Miranda was accused of attacking a young woman. When the police questioned him, he confessed to the crime. At Miranda's trial, his defense lawyer argued that his confession was not admissible as evidence because Miranda had not known about his right to a lawyer and his right not to speak. Still, Miranda was convicted, and he appealed.

In 1966, in *Miranda v. Arizona*, the Supreme Court ruled that the confession could not be used as evidence since Miranda had not been told his rights. After that, the police were required to recite the Miranda warning before questioning a suspect. The statement must have these key elements: the right to remain silent and the right to an attorney. The right to remain silent is guaranteed by the Fifth Amendment, which states that no one needs to be a witness against him- or herself. The right to an attorney, or counsel, is addressed in the Sixth Amendment. Answering basic questions such as one's name and address is not included in the Miranda rights.

Assistance of a Defense Attorney

And to have the Assistance of Counsel for his defence

In British common law, people accused of certain major crimes were not allowed counsel, or a lawyer to defend them. However, those accused of less serious crimes could hire counsel. Most likely, at the time the Bill of Rights was ratified, the phrase above meant that if the accused wanted a lawyer and could pay for one, he or she had the right to counsel. Therefore, wealthy defendants had a great advantage over those unable to afford a lawyer. This idea would change greatly over the years. Today, everyone has the right to an attorney in a criminal trial, whether the person can afford one or not. If a person can't afford to hire a private lawyer, the government appoints a public defender to take the case.

All Americans on trial for crimes are entitled to an attorney. Public defenders should provide a level of representation equal to that given by a private attorney.

CHAPTER FOUR

THE BILL OF RIGHTS IN ACTION

Like all of the amendments and the Constitution itself, the Sixth Amendment was just a group of ideas until it was exercised in the courtroom. When the justice system began applying these words to court cases, the amendment's complexity started to reveal itself. The Supreme Court ultimately decides how these concepts affect court decisions and people's lives.

The Supreme Court

The Supreme Court is the most powerful court in the United States. Established by Article III of the U.S. Constitution, it is the head of

Located in Washington, D.C., this building has housed the Supreme Court since 1935. Sixteen marble columns are found at the main entrance. Above the entrance appears the motto "Equal Justice Under Law."

the judicial branch of the federal government. The Supreme Court has nine judges, called justices, one of whom is the chief justice. Supreme Court justices are not elected. The judges are appointed by the president and approved by the Senate. They serve on the Court for life unless they resign.

Supreme Court justices study the parts of the Constitution that relate to each case. Then they decide how the Constitution applies to the case. The Court is in session from October to late June. Although thousands of cases are presented to the Court each year, only a few are taken on. The justices choose to hear the cases that have the greatest impact on the lives of Americans. Justices do not need to be in total agreement about decisions in cases. Some outcomes are decided by just one vote.

Federal Law Versus State Law

The amendments in the Bill of Rights are guarantees by the federal government. One of Madison's proposed amendments attempted to extend federal law so that it also applied to the states. It said, "No state shall violate the equal rights of conscience, or the freedom of the press, or the trial by jury in criminal cases." This amendment was rejected.

What's Behind the Name?

When a case goes to trial, it is labeled using the names of the people or groups involved in the matter. Often, the label will follow the format "plaintiff versus defendant." The person accusing is the plaintiff and the person being accused is the defendant. In a criminal case, the state government or a representative of the state government is usually named as the plaintiff. If a criminal case begins in federal court, the United States is listed as the plaintiff.

If the defendant loses, the party may file an appeal claiming that the court made an error or unjustly reached its decision. A higher court then reviews the case. The appeal trial may receive a new name. It will list the name of the person or party appealing first (usually it is the party that lost the first case) and then the name of the other party that had won. For example, in the case *Pointer v. Texas*, Pointer appealed the case after the trial court ruled in Texas's favor.

If a constitutional question is involved, the court decision may be appealed directly to the U.S. Supreme Court.

Anti-Federalists were cautious about allowing federal law to overshadow state law. The message at the time was clear: state criminal procedure did not have to agree with federal criminal procedure.

However, the differences between some state and federal laws could not remain. Some rights needed to be honored by all states. After the American Civil War, three amendments were ratified to guarantee African Americans citizenship and the rights that accompany it. It was necessary for the federal government to impose laws on the states that had formerly allowed slavery. One of these, the Fourteenth Amendment, promised:

> No State shall make or enforce any law which shall abridge the privileges or immunities of citizens of the United States; nor shall any State deprive any person of life, liberty, or property,

without due process of law; nor to deny to any person within its jurisdiction the equal protection of the laws.

Called the due process clause, the Fourteenth Amendment says that a state cannot deny anyone's rights without due process of law. Parts of the Sixth Amendment include due process procedures, such as notice of the accusation and selection of an impartial jury. The amendment's equal protection clause guarantees that everyone is protected equally under the law. In the twentieth century, the Fourteenth Amendment would be used to extend most parts of the Sixth Amendment to the states.

As depicted in *Harper's Weekly* in May 1873, loved ones carry the victims of the Colfax Massacre home. The incident called into question the authority of federal law versus state law.

The Supreme Court did not always agree that federal law should overshadow state law. A late-nineteenth-century case illustrates resistance to federal authority. On April 13, 1873, a large group of black men gathered in front of a courthouse in Colfax, Louisiana, to protest an election. An armed militia made up of white men attacked, killing over one hundred protesters. This event is sometimes called the Colfax Massacre.

Charges were filed against two of the militiamen. They were not charged with murder, but with stopping the protesters from assembling, bearing arms, and using free speech. According to federal law, these rights are guaranteed in the Bill of Rights. The case, *United States v. Cruikshank*, was brought before the Supreme Court in 1874 and decided in 1875. The Court maintained that the defendants' crimes against the plaintiffs involved state, not federal, laws. Therefore, the state would need to issue punishment. The Supreme Court argued that the Bill of Rights did not apply to the states unless the states chose to adopt it. Chief Justice Morrison R. Waite was quite clear in the Court's statement:

> We have in our political system a government of the United States and a government of each of the several States. Each one of these governments is distinct from the others, and each has citizens of its own who owe it allegiance, and whose rights, within its jurisdiction, it must protect. The same person may be at the same time a citizen of the United States and a citizen of a State, but his rights of citizenship under one of these governments will be different from those he has under the other.

The Court handed down this decision despite the existence of the Fourteenth Amendment. The views of the Court changed as the Court itself changed over the years. Retirements and deaths of justices brought new justices and new ideas to the Court.

The 1965 Supreme Court case described at the beginning of this book, *Pointer v. Texas*, is an example of the Court imposing the Bill of Rights on state law. In this case, there was a question about the Sixth Amendment right to confront a witness. Justice John Harlan was unhappy that the court "increasingly subjects state legal processes to enveloping federal judicial authority." However, Justice Arthur Goldberg stated that extending the Bill of Rights was not meant to grow federal power but "rather to limit the power of both federal and state governments in favor of safeguarding the fundamental rights and liberties of the individual."

Landmark Sixth Amendment Supreme Court Cases

As court cases came before different Supreme Court justices, their interpretations of the Sixth Amendment better defined certain constitutional ideas. The following court cases answered some important questions and helped to shape the Sixth Amendment.

How Much Time Is "Speedy"?

Willie Mae Barker was arrested for murder in 1958. However, he was not brought to trial until 1963. The reasons for this delay included a witness's illness and the wait for a decision in his partner's trial for the same crime. Barker was eventually found guilty once he stood trial. He asked for an appeal because he had not had a "speedy trial."

Barker v. Wingo was brought before the Supreme Court in 1972. The Court ruled that Barker's right to a speedy trial had not been violated. First, he did not demand his right until several years had passed.

Second, the justices concluded that a set amount of time could not be applied to the term "speedy." They outlined factors that other courts could use to define "speedy," including the amount of time, the reason for the delay, whether the defendant claimed the right, and whether time affects the outcome of the case.

What If a Public Trial Harms the Defense?

Sheppard v. Maxwell was a case in which the Supreme Court overturned a lower court's decision due to the media's influence. Sam Sheppard was put on trial for killing his wife. The television, radio, and newspapers portrayed Sheppard as guilty before his trial was complete. In 1966, the Supreme Court justices ruled that the case should have been delayed or moved so that the public, and the jury, would not unfairly judge Sheppard.

What Does an Impartial Jury Look Like?

This question was addressed in the case *Taylor v. Louisiana* (1975). Billy Taylor was convicted of kidnapping by an all-male jury. At that time in Louisiana, women did not have to serve on a jury unless they asked to participate. Taylor's defense attorney stated that his conviction was unconstitutional because his jury did not represent his community, which included women. The U.S. Supreme Court agreed, and the state was forced to change its jury selection process.

Should an Undercover Witness Be Cross-Examined?

In 1955, Albert Roviaro was convicted of selling drugs. Evidence of his guilt was provided by an undercover informant known as John Doe. Using a recording device, the informant provided evidence that Roviaro had sold him drugs. The government would not provide basic information about John Doe, including his real name. They argued that the

Potential jurors are selected from voter registration records. Attorneys for both sides ask jurors questions, or provide questions for the judge to ask, to determine whether the jurors are unbiased.

informant could not aid them again if his identity became known. Roviaro was convicted on Doe's evidence. Roviaro took his appeal to the U.S. Supreme Court and won. In *Roviaro v. United States*, the Court overturned the conviction because Roviaro's defense had not been able to cross-examine the witness.

Who Has the Right to Counsel?

In 1934, John Johnson was arrested in South Carolina for using counterfeit (fake) money. Though convicted, he appealed because he had not had legal counsel. Johnson did not have the money to hire an attorney.

The Supreme Court overturned the decision in *Johnson v. Zerbst*. This case made it mandatory for all defendants in federal criminal trials to be informed that they have the right to counsel. If defendants do not have money, the federal government must provide an attorney. The right to counsel was expanded to state courts in response to another case, *Gideon v. Wainwright*, in 1963.

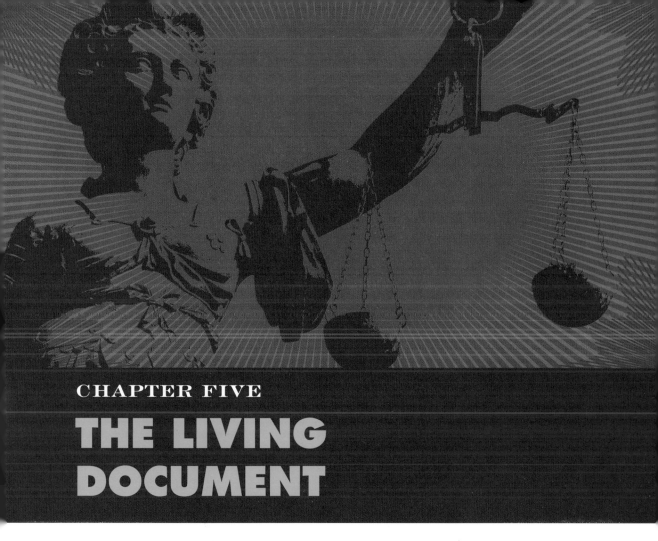

CHAPTER FIVE

THE LIVING DOCUMENT

T he U.S. Constitution is sometimes called the "living constitution." This label might seem strange at first. But in a way, the
Constitution is very much alive. The U.S. Constitution has
changed over the years with the additions of amendments. The process
required to adopt a new amendment ensures that only the most desired
and necessary additions are ratified.

The Ratification Process

The first step of ratification begins with a bill proposed to Congress.
Two-thirds of each house of Congress—the Senate and the House

of Representatives—needs to vote in favor of the amendment. Often, changes are made to the wording of the bill during this time. If the amendment gains the support of Congress, it is then passed on to each state legislature or a special state convention. Three-fourths of the states

The Nineteenth Amendment, which guarantees women the right to vote, was ratified on August 18, 1920. In this photo, supporters of women's suffrage watch Kentucky governor Edwin P. Morrow sign the amendment.

(or thirty-eight states) are needed for ratification. Over ten thousand amendments have been introduced in Congress since 1789, and just twenty-seven have been adopted. The Twenty-Seventh Amendment was ratified in 1992.

Current and Future Challenges

Americans' understanding of the Constitution's meaning has changed since the Constitutional Convention. The Bill of Rights works differently in our lives than it did in the lives of the early Americans. For example, the right to counsel in the 1800s was interpreted very differently from the right to an attorney today. Sweeping changes in the United States—such as the abolition of slavery and the rights of women—have had a great impact on this historical document as well.

Many Supreme Court justices follow a certain philosophy when defining the concepts of the Constitution. Some make decisions based on how they think the Founding Fathers interpreted the words. Others follow constitutional decisions made in the past, similar to the tradition of common law. Still others believe the meaning of the Constitution must change as the lives of Americans change. In recent years, Court

decisions have better defined and challenged past definitions of the rights in the Sixth Amendment. Read the cases that follow and reflect on your constitutional philosophy. If you were a justice, how would you have decided?

Seated at a table alone, Sonia Sotomayor faces questioning by the U.S. Senate during her confirmation hearings. The senators determined she was suitable to become a U.S. Supreme Court justice in 2009.

Lab Reports as Testimonial Evidence

Luis Melendez-Diaz was arrested in Massachusetts for possessing and selling drugs. The bags in which he kept the drugs were sent to a laboratory to be tested. The substance inside the bags was identified as cocaine in written reports from the laboratory. Melendez-Diaz was convicted, but he appealed. In *Melendez-Diaz v. Massachusetts* (2008/2009), his defense argued that the written statements from the drug lab were not a constitutional substitute for a witness. Melendez-Diaz did not have the chance to confront and cross-examine the lab technicians.

The majority of the Supreme Court agreed with Melendez-Diaz. They defined evidence like the lab report as "testimonial" evidence. The Court said that for testimonial evidence to be used, the defense must have the right to cross-examine those that prepare it. Previously, scientific evidence such as lab reports had been allowed as evidence without cross-examination.

Melendez-Diaz v. Massachusetts will likely have important consequences for the future of trials. Every drug test, every DNA report, and other forms of testimonial evidence may need to be accompanied by the people who prepare them. Some people are concerned that scientists and

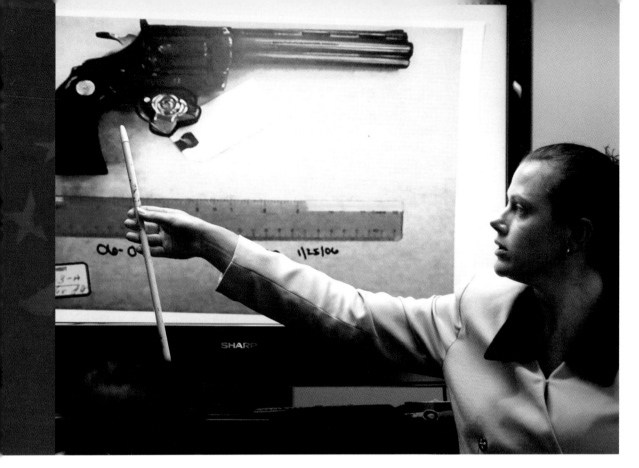

A forensic scientist explains tests that she performed on a gun featured in a murder trial. Scientists from police crime labs provide important DNA evidence used in trials.

lab technicians will be spending less time in their places of work and more time at lengthy trials in order to fulfill the confrontation clause.

Children as Witnesses

In 1990, the Court handed down a historic decision regarding children as witnesses. *Maryland v. Craig* involved a six-year-old child who was abused by a teacher, Sandra Craig. At the trial, the child gave testimony in a room that was separate from the courtroom. The testimony was televised live in the courtroom. Though the child could not see anyone in the courtroom, the defense could see the child, question the child, and receive answers.

Try, Try Again—The 27th Amendment

The Twenty-seventh Amendment, the most recent addition to the Constitution, has roots in one of the original twelve amendments written by James Madison. It states: "No law, varying the compensation for the services of the Senators and Representatives, shall take effect, until an election of Representatives shall have intervened."

This measure provides a check on congressional salaries. If congressional representatives vote in favor of a raise for themselves, the raise will not occur until after the next election. Therefore, if people do not agree that their representatives deserve a raise, they can vote them out of office before payment is received.

Madison was surprised and disappointed that the amendment was not passed with the others. He believed strongly in the idea. In fact, while he was a representative in the Virginia legislature, he never accepted a pay raise. In 1992, Madison's amendment finally became law.

The prosecution made this arrangement to keep the child from experiencing distress as a result of seeing the teacher. The court convicted Craig. She appealed, saying that her right to confront her accuser had been violated.

The Supreme Court did not agree with Craig. In a close decision, the justices decided that there were "certain narrow circumstances" in which confrontation is not absolutely guaranteed. In this case, the defense was able to cross-examine the child. The jury could observe the child giving testimony and assess the child's credibility. The Court decided that it was more important to protect the child's well-being than to allow the defendant to see her accuser face-to-face.

War, Enemy Soldiers, and Guantánamo

The Sixth Amendment guarantees citizens a trial by jury in the place where the crime was committed. Are these same rights guaranteed in times of war? Recent wars have caused U.S. citizens to wonder what rights are owed to people who are enemies of the United States.

During the war in Afghanistan, the United States flew enemy soldiers, one of whom was an American citizen, to Guantánamo Bay in Cuba and to the United States. The soldiers were put in jail to await trials by military tribunals. Tribunals may hear secret evidence and testimony that the accused may never know about.

A detainee is led from a questioning session back to his quarters at a camp in Guantánamo Bay, Cuba.

Some people are outraged by these kinds of trials. Others think only Americans loyal to the nation are guaranteed the rights promised in the Constitution. Many questions remain: Do American criminal procedures have a place in times of war? Are there circumstances in which constitutional rights should be taken away?

The Sixth Amendment: Today and Tomorrow

Where do you see the Sixth Amendment in your life? Chances are, you will not face a criminal trial yourself, but a friend or family member might. The Sixth Amendment is in place for anyone accused of a crime in the United States. For a person who believes he or she is innocent, it gives that person a fighting chance to prove his or her innocence. The Sixth Amendment is there when citizens need it, along with the rest of the Bill of Rights of the U.S. Constitution.

AMENDMENTS TO THE U.S. CONSTITUTION

First Amendment (proposed 1789; ratified 1791): Freedom of religion, speech, press, assembly, and petition

Second Amendment (proposed 1789; ratified 1791): Right to bear arms

Third Amendment (proposed 1789; ratified 1791): No quartering of soldiers in private houses in times of peace

Fourth Amendment (proposed 1789; ratified 1791): Interdiction of unreasonable search and seizure; requirement of search warrants

Fifth Amendment (proposed 1789; ratified 1791): Indictments; due process; self-incrimination; double jeopardy; eminent domain

Sixth Amendment (proposed 1789; ratified 1791): Right to a fair and speedy public trial; notice of accusations; confronting one's accuser; subpoenas; right to counsel

Seventh Amendment (proposed 1789; ratified 1791): Right to a trial by jury in civil cases

Eighth Amendment (proposed 1789; ratified 1791): No excessive bail and fines; no cruel or unusual punishment

Ninth Amendment (proposed 1789; ratified 1791): Protection of unenumerated rights (rights inferred from other legal rights but that are not themselves coded or enumerated in written constitution and laws)

Tenth Amendment (proposed 1789; ratified 1791): Limits the power of the federal government

Eleventh Amendment (proposed 1794; ratified 1795): Sovereign immunity (immunity of states from suits brought by out-of-state citizens and foreigners living outside of states' borders)

Twelfth Amendment (proposed 1803; ratified 1804): Revision of presidential election procedures (electoral college)

Thirteenth Amendment (proposed 1865; ratified 1865): Abolition of slavery

Fourteenth Amendment (proposed 1866; ratified 1868): Citizenship; state due process; application of Bill of Rights to states; revision to apportionment of congressional representatives; denies public office to anyone who has rebelled against the United States

Fifteenth Amendment (proposed 1869; ratified 1870): Suffrage no longer restricted by race

Sixteenth Amendment (proposed 1909; ratified 1913): Allows federal income tax

Seventeenth Amendment (proposed 1912; ratified 1913): Direct election to the U.S. Senate by popular vote

Eighteenth Amendment (proposed 1917; ratified 1919): Prohibition of alcohol

Nineteenth Amendment (proposed 1919; ratified 1920): Women's suffrage

Twentieth Amendment (proposed 1932; ratified 1933): Term commencement for Congress (January 3) and president (January 20)

Twenty-first Amendment (proposed 1933; ratified 1933): Repeal of Eighteenth Amendment (Prohibition)

Twenty-second Amendment (proposed 1947; ratified 1951): Limits president to two terms

Twenty-third Amendment (proposed 1960; ratified 1961): Representation of the District of Colombia in electoral college

Twenty-fourth Amendment (proposed 1962; ratified 1964): Prohibition of restriction of voting rights due to nonpayment of poll taxes

Twenty-fifth Amendment (proposed 1965; ratified 1967): Presidential succession

Twenty-sixth Amendment (proposed 1971; ratified 1971): Voting age of eighteen

Twenty-seventh Amendment (proposed 1789; ratified 1992): Congressional compensation

Proposed but Unratified Amendments

Congressional Apportionment Amendment (proposed 1789; still technically pending): Apportionment of U.S. representatives

Titles of Nobility Amendment (proposed 1810; still technically pending): Prohibition of titles of nobility

Corwin Amendment (proposed 1861; still technically pending though superseded by Thirteenth Amendment): Preservation of slavery

Child Labor Amendment (proposed 1924; still technically pending): Congressional power to regulate child labor

Equal Rights Amendment (proposed 1972; expired): Prohibition of inequality of men and women

District of Columbia Voting Rights Amendment (proposed 1978; expired): District of Columbia voting rights

GLOSSARY

acquit To free or clear from a charge or accusation; to declare not guilty.

appeal To apply for review of a case to a higher court.

bias A personal judgment or preconceived opinion that prevents a person from impartially evaluating the facts in a case.

charter A written grant or guarantee of rights and privileges from an authority of a state or country.

convict To find guilty of a crime or offense after a trial.

cross-examine To question a witness who is testifying on behalf of the opposing party in a trial.

defendant The party against whom a criminal charge or civil claim is brought in court.

enact To make into law.

Federalist A supporter of a strong central government and weaker state governments; a supporter of the adoption of the Constitution written in 1787.

hearing A preliminary examination in criminal procedure.

hearsay Secondhand evidence in which the witness does not tell what he or she knows personally, but what someone else, not under oath, has said.

informant A person who gives information to the police about the criminal activities of others.

Parliament The supreme legislative body in Britain.

philosophy A study of the truths and principles of a particular area of experience; the basic beliefs, concepts, and attitudes of an individual or group.

plaintiff A person or party who brings a legal action or suit, making a charge of wrongdoing against another party.

prosecute To try a person in court for a civil or criminal offense.

ratify To approve formally.

subpoena An order of the court for a person to testify or to submit evidence, under penalty for failing to do so.

testify To give testimony (spoken or written declarations) or other evidence under oath.

tribunal A person or body of people that hears and decides disputes; a court or other forum of justice.

FOR MORE INFORMATION

James Madison Museum
129 Caroline Street
Orange, VA 22960-1532
(540) 672-1776
E-mail: info@jamesmadisonmus.org
Web site: http://www.jamesmadisonmus.org
Located in James Madison's home county, this museum commemorates the fourth
U.S. president and father of the Constitution.

Library and Archives Canada
395 Wellington Street
Ottawa, ON K1A 0N4
Canada
(613) 996-5115 or 1-866-578-7777
Web site: http://www.collectionscanada.gc.ca
This institution preserves and shares information about the most important historical
documents of Canada.

The National Archives and Records Administration
8601 Adelphi Road
College Park, MD 20740-6001
(866) 272-6272
Web site: http://www.archives.gov
The National Archives and Records Administration is the record keeper of the
United States. Valuable documents and records, including the Constitution, are pre-
served and made available to the public.

National Constitution Center

525 Arch Street
Independence Mall
Philadelphia, PA 19106
(866) 917-1787
Web site: http://www.constitutioncenter.org
The National Constitution Center is a museum dedicated to increasing public understanding of the U.S. Constitution.

Supreme Court of Canada

301 Wellington Street
Ottawa, ON K1A 0J1
Canada
(613) 995-4330 or 1-888-551-1185
E-mail: reception@scc-csc.gc.ca
Web site: http://www.scc-csc.gc.ca
This site contains information on Canada's judicial system and constitution.

Supreme Court of the United States

One First Street NE
Washington, DC 20543
(202) 479-3211
Web site: http://www.supremecourtus.gov
Find information about the judicial system of the United States, as well as information about visiting the Court.

United States House of Representatives

U.S. Capitol
Washington, DC 20515

(202) 224-3121

Web site: http://www.house.gov

Ask questions and send comments to U.S. representatives through this Web site.

United States Senate

U.S. Capitol

Washington, DC 20510

(202) 224-3121

Wcb sitc: http://www.scnatc.gov

Ask questions and submit comments regarding public policy issues or legislation to the U.S. senators.

Web Sites

Due to the changing nature of Internet links, Rosen Publishing has developed an online list of Web sites related to the subject of this book. This site is updated regularly. Please use this link to access the list:

http://www.rosenlinks.com/ausc/6th

FOR FURTHER READING

Burgan, Michael. *Miranda v. Arizona: The Rights of the Accused* (Snapshots in History). Minneapolis, MN: Compass Point Books, 2007.

Cefrey, Holly. *The United States Constitution and Early State Constitutions: Law and Order in the New Nation and States* (Life in the New American Nation). New York, NY: Rosen Publishing, 2004.

Cheney, Lynne V. *We the People: The Story of Our Constitution*. New York, NY: Simon & Schuster Books for Young Readers, 2008.

Fradin, Dennis B. *The Bill of Rights*. Tarrytown, NY: Marshall Cavendish Benchmark, 2009.

Freedman, Russell. *In Defense of Liberty: The Story of America's Bill of Rights*. New York, NY: Holiday House, 2003.

Fridell, Ron. *Gideon v. Wainwright: The Right to Free Counsel* (Supreme Court Milestones). Tarrytown, NY: Marshall Cavendish Benchmark, 2007.

Gold, Susan Dudley. *In Re Gault: Do Minors Have the Same Rights as Adults?* (Supreme Court Milestones). New York, NY: Marshall Cavendish Benchmark, 2008.

Graham, Amy. *A Look at the Bill of Rights: Protecting the Rights of Americans* (Constitution of the United States). Berkeley Heights, NJ: Enslow Publishers, 2008.

Hamilton, Alexander, James Madison, and John Jay. *The Federalist Papers*. New York, NY: Simon & Schuster, 2004.

Haugen, David M., and Susan Musser. *Criminal Justice* (Opposing Viewpoints Series). Detroit, MI: Greenhaven Press, 2009.

Hennessey, Jonathan, and Aaron McConnell. *The United States Constitution: A Graphic Adaptation*. New York, NY: Hill and Wang, 2008.

Labunski, Richard E. *James Madison and the Struggle for the Bill of Rights*. New York, NY: Oxford University Press, 2006.

Leavitt, Amie Jane. *The Bill of Rights in Translation: What It Really Means*. Mankato, MN: Capstone Press, 2009.

Lewis, Thomas T. *The U.S. Supreme Court*. Pasadena, CA: Salem Press, 2007.

Orr, Tamra. *Careers in the Court System* (Careers in Criminal Justice). New York, NY: Rosen Publishing Group, 2010.

Panchyk, Richard. *Our Supreme Court: A History with 14 Activities*. Chicago, IL: Chicago Review Press, 2007.

Ritchie, Donald A. *Our Constitution*. New York, NY: Oxford University Press, 2006.

Smith, Rich. *Sixth Amendment: The Right to a Fair Trial* (The Bill of Rights). Edina, MN: ABDO Publishing, 2008.

Sobel, Syl. *The Bill of Rights: Protecting Our Freedom Then and Now*. Hauppauge, NY: Barron's Educational Series, 2008.

Yero, Judith Lloyd. *The Bill of Rights* (American Documents). Washington, DC: National Geographic, 2006.

BIBLIOGRAPHY

Bent, Devin. "James Madison Proposes Bill of Rights." James Madison University. Retrieved March 1, 2010 (http://www.jmu.edu/madison/gpos225-madison2/madprobll.htm#opendoor).

Boston Massacre Historical Society. "The Summary of the Boston Massacre Trial." 2008. Retrieved February 14, 2010 (http://www.bostonmassacre.net/trial/trial-summary4.htm).

Breig, James. "All That is Substantial and Beneficial in a Trial by Jury." *Colonial Williamsburg Journal*, Spring 2008. Retrieved March 5, 2010 (http://www.history.org/Foundation/journal/Spring08/trials.cfm).

FindLaw.com. "U.S. Constitution: Sixth Amendment: Annotations." Retrieved February 5, 2010 (http://caselaw.lp.findlaw.com/data/Constitution/amendment06/01.html).

History.com. "The Continental Congress." Retrieved February 19, 2010 (http://www.history.com/topics/the-continental-congress).

Jefferson, Thomas. "Avalon Project—A Summary View of the Rights of British America." Lillian Goldman Law Library, Yale Law School. Retrieved February 17, 2010 (http://avalon.law.yale.edu/18th_century/jeffsumm.asp).

Justia.com. "*Taylor v. Louisiana*, 419 U.S. 522." Retrieved March 2, 2010 (http://supreme.justia.com/us/419/522).

Law Library—American Law and Legal Information. "*Johnson v. Zerbst*—Significance, Supreme Court Requires That Counsel Be Appointed, Federal Court of Appeals." Retrieved February 15, 2010 (http://law.jrank.org/pages/12973/Johnson-v-Zerbst.html).

Law Library—American Law and Legal Information. "*Pointer v. Texas*—Significance." Retrieved February 15, 2010 (http://law.jrank.org/pages/23888/Pointer-v-Texas-Significance.html).

Law Library—American Law and Legal Information. "*U.S. v. Cruikshank*: 1875—Supreme Court Delivers a Crushing Blow." Retrieved February 15, 2010 (http://law.jrank.org/pages/2631/U-S-v-Cruikshank-1875-Supreme-Court-Delivers-Crushing-Blow.html).

Lillian Goldman Law Library, Yale Law School. "Avalon Project—English Bill of Rights 1689." Retrieved February 15, 2010 (http://avalon.law.yale.edu/17th_century/england.asp).

Lillian Goldman Law Library, Yale Law School. "Avalon Project—Magna Carta 1215." Retrieved February 15, 2010 (http://avalon.law.yale.edu/medieval/magframe.asp).

Linder, Douglas O. "The Boston Massacre Trials: An Account." Famous Trials Web site, University of Missouri–Kansas City School of Law. 2001. Retrieved March 2, 2010 (http://www.law.umkc.edu/faculty/projects/ftrials/bostonmassacre/bostonaccount.html).

Milazzo, Paul, and Joseph J. Thorndike. "Tax History Museum: 1756–1776: The Seven Years War to the American Revolution." Tax History Project at Tax Analysts. Retrieved February 10, 2010 (http://www.taxanalysts.com/Museum/1756-1776.htm).

Mount, Steve. "The Administration of Justice Act—The U.S. Constitution Online." USConstitution.net. Retrieved February 20, 2010 (http://www.usconstitution.net/adminjustact.html).

The National Archives and Records Administration. "The Charters of Freedom: Bill of Rights." Retrieved February 16, 2010 (http://www.archives.gov/exhibits/charters/bill_of_rights.html).

The National Archives and Records Administration. "Featured Documents: The Magna Carta." Retrieved February 2, 2010 (http://www.archives.gov/exhibits/featured_documents/magna_carta).

Oyez.org. "*Sheppard v. Maxwell*, U.S. Supreme Court Case Summary & Oral Argument." Retrieved February 7, 2010 (http://www.oyez.org/cases/1960-1969/1965/1965_490).

Roland, Jon, ed. "The Declaratory Act, March 18, 1766." Constitution Society. Retrieved February 17, 2010 (http://www.constitution.org/bcp/decl_act.htm).

Rowley, Charles K. "The Thought of James Madison." The Locke Institute, 1999. Retrieved March 3, 2010 (http://www.thelocke institute.org/journals/luminary_v2_n1_p4.html).

Time.com. "The Supreme Court: Now Comes the Sixth Amendment." April 16, 1965. Retrieved February 12, 2010 (http://www.time.com/time/magazine/article/0,9171,841844,00.html).

U.S. Government Printing Office. "Ben's Guide: The Articles of Confederation." February 26, 2003. Retrieved February 24, 2010 (http://bensguide.gpo.gov/9-12/documents/articles/index.html).

Uzgalis, William. "John Locke." *Stanford Encyclopedia of Philosophy*, May 5, 2007. Retrieved March 10, 2010 (http://plato.stanford.edu/archives/fall2009/entries/locke/).

INDEX

About the Author

Therese Shea is the editor and author of many educational nonfiction books, including several on the Bill of Rights, the Constitution, and the U.S. government. A graduate of Providence College, the author holds an M.A. in English education from the State University of New York at Buffalo. She lives in Buffalo, New York, with her husband, Mark, an attorney who helped clarify legal concepts throughout the writing of this book.

Photo Credits

Cover (left) Daniel Gluskoter-Pool/Getty Images; cover (middle) Doug Pizac-Pool/Getty Images; cover (right) Mario Tama/Getty Images; p. 1 (top) © www.istockphoto.com/Tom Nulens; p. 1 (bottom) © www.istockphoto.com/Lee Pettet; p. 3 © www.istockphoto.com/Nic Taylor; pp. 4–5 Photos.com/Thinkstock; pp. 8, 19, 24, 33, 41 © www.istockphoto.com/arturbo; pp. 10–11, 26 Bridgeman Art Library/Getty Images; p. 13 Mario Tama/Getty Images; pp. 16–17, 36 MPI/Getty Images; p. 20 SuperStock/Getty Images; p. 23 http://www.ourdocuments.gov; p. 28 Fuse/Getty Images; p. 30 © www.istockphoto.com/Kirby Hamilton; pp. 32, 46 © AP Images; p. 34 Hemera/Thinkstock; p. 40 Image Source/Getty Images; pp. 42–43 Library of Congress Prints and Photographs Division; pp. 44–45 Joshua Roberts/Bloomberg/Getty Images; p. 48 Chris Hondros/Getty Images.

Editor: Andrea Sclarow; Photo Researcher: Amy Feinberg